<u>HOW TO ANALYZE</u>

<u>PEOPLE</u>

An Ideal Book for

Understanding Different

Personalities

Aiden MCcoy

© *2015*

Disclaimer

Table of Contents

Intoduction

It is truly said," Beauty lies in the eyes of the beholder". A popular English idiom states, "Don't judge a book by its cover." The main question why these lines are mentioned is for the simple reason that people arrive at a quick decision about another person. You may meet a person for the first time, but how do you come to know what kind of a person he is?

This question is answered by the fact of judging and analyzing people. Some people believe that one can understand another person's personality on the basis of his body language, his walk, or even facial features. While it is absolutely true, still in order to analyze the personality of another human being, you need to explore a deeper meaning about many factors other than those which have been mentioned.

Before analyzing someone, we must realize that there are three kinds of people – visual, auditory and kinesthetic people. The categories of people will be explained in detail in the EBook. It is essential to study the communication process – verbal as well as non-verbal – to understand a human being's personality or character.

The term 'Personality' refers to differences among people in the context of behavioral patterns, emotion and cognition. Temperament is a quality that is considered to be the precursor to an individual's personality. People are categorized into two groups: extroverts and introverts. Extroverts tend to manifest in actions of being talkative, adventurous, assertive and outgoing. Introverts exhibit a solitary and reserved behavior. Theorists have argued over the topic of understanding people from a different culture. Some think that, personality is a derivation of an individual's culture; therefore it is meaningless to understand cross-cultures' personality. On the contrary, others feel that common elements are present in every culture and an effort is made to apply the principle of "the Big Five" to demonstrate personalities in different cultures. The Big Five theory studies the different traits associated to an individual's personality: openness, extraversion, conscientiousness, agreeableness, and emotionality or neuroticism.

Personality judgment refers to the process where people understand an individual's personality by receiving specific information about the other person, or meeting him/her personally. Through this EBook, readers will get an idea about the factors required to analyze the personality of another human being. This EBook aims to help people understand how they can maintain a good relationship by learning the art of analyzing the personality of another individual accurately.

The First Impressions

It is truly said, "The first impression is the last impression".

The accuracy of judging an individual's personality is based on three important perspectives of pragmatism, realism and constructivism.

Psychologists maintain that first impression refers to an event where a person meets another person for the first time and creates a mental picture of the other person. The accuracy in creating a first impression is based on a variety of characteristics: race, age, culture, gender, language, accent, physical appearance, voice, posture, and the time taken to form an impression. The first impressions have a great influence on individuals as to how they are viewed and treated in the various contexts of life.

A quick glance, generally one-tenth of a second, is enough for a person to form a first impression. The other person creates an opinion based on the appearance, body language, mannerisms, demeanor and the way a person dresses. We meet many people every day; thus, forming a new impression about ourselves in other's minds. It is impossible to reverse the effect of a first impression; therefore, it is very important to create a good impression as it sets the tone for the future of a relationship, whether social or professional.

Listed below are some important factors to be kept in mind when you're going to meet someone for the first time:

• Be punctual: It is a poor excuse if you reach the meeting venue late. It is better to reach little early. Keep enough time in hand to manage traffic or detours.

• Be Natural: A wrong impression is one where a person appears to be uncomfortable or edgy. A calm and confident approach lays a strong foundation to create a good first impression. This attitude makes the other person comfortable too.

- Dress appropriately: It is not necessary to dress up as a model, when you are meeting for the first time. The other person does not know you; so the objective should be to create a decent impression about yourself in the other's mind. Dress according to the occasion. If the event is a business meeting, don an appropriate business attire such as a suit, blazer. For social events, give attention to the traditions or cultural norms of the host and dress accordingly. Neat and tidy attire creates an excellent first impression. Present yourself in a comfortable and confident way in the event.

- Groom yourself properly: Small habits such as a haircut, clipped nails and absence of mouth odor are some of the grooming tips you can follow when preparing yourself to meet someone.

- Sport a Smiling Face: A warm smile creates an excellent first impression. Greet everyone with a smile on your face, but do not overdo it.

- Openness: Body language is a great element of creating first impressions. Non verbal actions and gestures speak louder than the actual words. Maintaining eye contact while speaking, firm handshake, and standing tall are some of the gestures that help create a good first impression as you appear to others as a confident person. Awareness about the nervous habits will help you control the nervous actions such as biting nails, rubbing sweaty palms and many others.

- Small Conversations: Striking a meaningful conversation follows the give-and-take policy. Prepare a list of questions you want to ask the person you are going to meet. Or, attempt to learn about that person by letting him talk first. If some common point arises, you can talk further.

conversation. The basic art of active listening is very simple. The process includes the actions where you listen, make suggestions or comments, repeat key points, and ask reasonable questions to further the discussion.

The aspect of questioning plays an important role in conversations. Usually, people are not confident about what type questions they should ask. One must avoid asking stereotypical questions and ask something worthwhile to add to the conversation.

The major mistake people make is dominating the conversation. It is hard to understand when you are dominating a conversation. Intentionally, you may be simply starting a conversation, but in the end it may turn out that you are the one who is talking the most, maybe because you are excited or nervous about the topic.

After discussing about the common mistakes, I would like to focus on the value of good questioning. Good questions are a symbol of productivity, creativity, positive attitude and can help us achieve our goals. The process of effective questioning also requires the art of effective listening.

The benefits of effective questioning include:

- Meaningful connections with clients
- Proper understanding of the client's problems
- Effective work culture in the organization
- Motivate employees to assume responsibility
- A better collection of information.
- Improvement in negotiation skills
- Reduction in communication errors
- Give valuable feedback
- Share your ideas and experience

So, what do you mean by an effective question? These are questions that invite thought provoking and powerful reactions. They are open-ended in nature and a good source of collecting useful information. One must remember to wait patiently for the answer to these kinds of questions, as people may become defensive in some cases.

Rather than making assumptions you must find what the other person knows in relation to the topic being talked about. For instance, "How do you see the problem?" Powerful questions improve the process of communication as well as the understanding of the other person. Such questions are used to conduct interviews, settle negotiations and in problem-solving decisions. Examples include, "What do you make of the problem?", "What do you think about the strategy?", "What seems to be your obstacle?", and many others. Questions related to outcomes or results give an idea about the way how to approach a work or activity. Examples include, "What is your plan?", "What do you want?", and many others. The questions such as "What will you do?", "What is your next move?" determine the actions that must be taken to achieve a goal.

Although we have a number of reasons for asking specific questions the information we receive depends on what type of question is asked.

The simplest form of questions is classified as open-ended or close-ended.

Close- ended questions invite a definite answer with a short focus, either the answer is right or it is wrong. Close-ended questions usually have a limited answer; it is appropriate to begin a conversation by asking such questions to collect facts and encourage participation. Examples include," What is your name?", "Would you like to have a cup of tea?", and many such questions that can invite a response of only one word.

On the contrary, open-ended questions invite longer responses involving information and creativity. The open-ended questions are further classified as loaded or leading questions, recall and response questions, and rhetorical questions.

A leading or loaded question subtly guides the response in a particular direction. For instance, the question of 'How are you getting on with the new vendor system?' This question will prompt another question on how to acquaint them with the new system. Subtly, it communicates that maybe they are not in favor of the new system or maybe they have some kind of objection to it.

Children are susceptible to such types of questions and take the initiative of answering a question from the parent. For instance, "Did you have a good day at school?" will guide the child to think about the good experiences in the school that took place during the day. The leading questions are important for the purpose of giving a shape to the conversation as the response to the first question will lead to asking the second question.

Some questions are classified as recall questions as they can be answered by recalling information based on facts or simple memory. An example of this type of question is, "What is the capital of the United States?" Process questions are those involving a deep analysis or thought process. Example of such questions includes, "What are the advantages and disadvantages of parental control software?"

Rhetorical Questions are a type of open-ended questions asked to create an impact and do not require a definite answer. Examples include, "Aren't you ashamed of yourself?", "Can't you do anything right?", and many others. Speakers use rhetorical questions while giving presentations in order to motivate the listeners to think. Lecturers, priests, politician and other personalities may use such type of questions to address large audiences to attract their attention. These questions do not require an answer but trigger the people to think thus creating uninterrupted attention to what is being said.

The process of funneling includes a number of questions that can be asked based on the response. The questions are restrictive in nature, beginning with open-ended questions and ending with closed-ended questions. Examples of such questions include:

"When exactly did you reach home?"

"What did you do after reaching home?"

"What time did you have dinner?"

"Will you go to the office tomorrow?"

Funneling questions can be asked in another way, beginning with close-ended questions and ending with open-ended questions. A counselor usually uses these techniques to extract maximum information.

As we have listed the various types of questions that one can ask, we will have a look at the types of the responses that will be attracted for different type of questions.

- An honest and direct response is the one desired by the person asking the question. A speaker loves to hear an honest response to the question.

- A person may lie while responding a question. The questioner may be smart to decipher a lie on the basis of the plausibility of response, but due to the non-verbal communication used immediately before telling a lie, as well as after responding to the question.

- A respondent may give an answer that is completely out of the context, i.e. irrelevant or unconnected. This kind of response is given in an attempt to alter the topic of discussion. The best option will be to rephrase the question in such cases to elicit an appropriate response.

- Often people are selective about answering questions. They tend to answer the questions according to their comfort level and choose to avoid uncomfortable questions.

- Politicians are usually associated with the trait of avoiding the answer. When a journalist asks a difficult or a disturbing question that may elicit a negative effect, they use the tactics of avoiding it by asking another question or mentioning some positive idea related to the topic of discussion.

- The process of stalling a response is one where the respondent requires some time before answering the question. Similar to avoiding an answer, the respondent asks another question to buy more time.

- People often give distorted responses on the basis of how they perceive stereotypes, social norms and other types of bias. In such cases, respondents do not understand that their responses are biased or a mere form of exaggeration.

- If a person does not wish to answer, he may simply refuse to offer a response. This can be done by staying silent or by stating, "I will not answer the question."

The skill of effective listening requires continuous nurturing along with needs development. For instance, lawyers use this art at a very minimal level. An effective lawyer must maintain high quality listening skills as well as effective questioning skills in order to establish a trustworthy relationship with his client.

There are several factors that may hamper a person from practicing the art of effective listening. These factors include:

- A temptation to dominate or control the conversation.

- You might wish to exhibit your skills and intelligence, so you tell the answer before the other person has completed asking the question.

- Listening may allow the other person to express his ideas and emotions which may be beyond your comfort level.

A complete understanding of the statements spoken by the other person will result in a logical deduction instead of answering the question immediately; this is the key of effective listening and problem solving techniques.

One must understand the various levels of the process of effective listening:

Level 1

The first level of effective listening is useful when you collect information such as receiving directions, or placing an order in a store. In this level, you must focus your attention on how you are affected by the words spoken by the other person without too much attention to the person who is speaking. The focus is on your thoughts, ideas, judgments, problems, conclusions, and emotions. You must not think about the emotions of the person who is speaking.

Level 2

This level deeply focuses on the speaker of the conversation. In this level, we may not be aware about the context of the topic. We observe what is being said and how the speaker is saying and the non-verbal part as well. We practice the art of listening with full awareness about the other person speaking. We listen with attention about the things they attach importance to and what makes them feel happy or sad. We do not involve the process of judgment on this particular level. We do not concentrate on planning as to how to react. Rather, our response is affected by what we hear in reality.

Level 3

This level is a combination of skills used in the previous two levels. In this level, we add to the conversation, gather information, create awareness about the context, and study the effect of the conversation on all members. We also focus our attention to our intuition and all other senses. We observe the nonverbal language and the atmosphere created due to the conversation. This information facilitates in asking effective questions on the relevant topic.

The various listening skills contributing to effective questioning are as follows:

- Articulation is the result of paying attention and being aware of listening to what is being said. A successful articulation is one wherein people share their opinions and ideas without the involvement of any kind of judgment. Articulating a statement acknowledges a person that he is being heard.

- You must develop a sense of curiosity. An assumption about the next statement is a wrong approach. Be curious to know what attracts the other person to talk to you. What is their motivation behind meeting you?

- **Clarification** is a combined process of questioning and articulating what you hear. By the means of questions you fill the gaps and give a sense that you are listening attentively. It is essential to clarify if the other person is vague. You can help me to clarify the meaning of the sentence by giving suggestions. For instance, "Here is what I feel you are speaking about. Is it correct?"

- **Silence** A good listener must give enough time to the speaker for answering the questions raised. A few minutes of silence give the impression that you are listening.

Discovering Patterns

Human behavior changes throughout the entire lifetime of an individual. It includes our actions based on various factors such as genetics, faith, social norms and attitude. The traits of an individual creates an impact on his behavior. Traits are the distinguishing characteristics of an individual which result in different behavior and actions performed by each person. People are supposed to follow certain social norms and behave according to the acceptable standards of the society. Different behaviors are perceived to be acceptable or unacceptable in different cultural societies. Faith is guided by the philosophy and religion of the person; it is the foundation of the manner in which a person thinks and this results in the different kinds of behavior. Attitude is defined as "the degree to which the person has a favorable or an unfavorable evaluation of the behavior in question." The attitude of an individual reflects the kind of behavior displayed during specific situations. The behavi̇ ̇ ̇ ̇ttern of an individual is influenced by that ̇ ̇ ude.

The detailed analysis of a personality depends upon the essential view that each and every person is similar in some aspects, yet a slight difference occurs in other aspects. Psychologists have mutually agreed on the following definition of the term 'Personality'-" Personality is that pattern of characteristic thoughts, feelings, and behaviors that distinguish one person from another and that persists over time and situations."

There have been many theories that have helped in analyzing the personality of an individual.

Trait theories

The trait theories are based on these assumptions – a) Traits vary among individuals, b) An individual exhibits relatively stable traits over time, c) Traits influence the behavior pattern of an individual, d) Traits are constant; they do not change, and e) Traits are usually bipolar, i.e. they vary between one extreme and the other.

Presently, the Big Five Factor theory of studying personality has gained worldwide recognition. A famous psychologist named Lewis Goldberg propounded the model of five-dimensional personality that was called the "Big Five"

It is essential to understand the five major factors that influence the personality of an individual. These factors include:

- Openness to Experience: This factor refers to the ability to be independent, creative and inclined towards variety rather than conforming, being practical, and inclined towards routine.

- The factor of conscientiousness refers to an individual's tendency of being careful, methodical, organized, and disciplined rather than carelessness, being impulsive, and disorganized

- Extraversion is a factor to study an individual who is sociable, affectionate, and fun-loving compared to someone who has a tendency of being reserved, retiring, and somber.

- The factor of Agreeableness is the tendency of an individual to be trustful, helpful, and softhearted, vs. uncooperative, suspicious, and ruthless.

- Neuroticism studies the tendency of feeling insecure, self-pity, and anxious vs. self-satisfaction, calmness, and a sense of security.

Traits are regarded as generalizations that may not always reflect the true behavior of an individual. Genetic influences play an equally important role in determining the personality of an individual. The effect of genetic influences is analyzed by studying a pair of twins as they share the same environment. Genetics develops the instincts of an individual, i.e. a behavioral pattern practiced without any thought preconceived thoughts and which cannot change by learning. The common examples of instinctive behavior include patterns which include the response to a specific stimulus. For instance, a cockroach flies across the room in search of a dark corner once the lights are switched on. Genetic information determines behavior in the best manner when the environment of an individual undergoes very little change across generations, or with reference to the communication process it is a behavior when a person is sending or receiving unambiguous messages.

Type theories

The classification of people based on the psychological development is studied under the type theories. Different people are classified into various types based on the varied traits and behavior exhibited by them. For instance, the two common types of personality, according to these theories, are extroverts and introverts.

Introversion and extroversion are psychological orientations in relation to two forms of functions:

The functions of perception, i.e. intuition and sensation. These functions are based on the trust in concrete, absolute, and sensory-oriented situations called facts rather than abstract ideas and imaginary situations.

The judging functions involve expressing feelings based on a rational approach and thinking. It means the decisions are made based on logical deductions. The effects of actions on people have not been taken into consideration.

A popular psychologist, Meyer Friedman propounded the Type A and Type B personality theory in 1950. The theory stated that, " intense, hard-driving Type A personalities had a higher risk of coronary disease because they are "stress junkies. Type B people, on the other hand, tended to be relaxed, less competitive, and lower in risk." There also exists a combination of both personalities referred to as the type AB.

The theory states "Type A" individuals are organized, disciplined, ambitious, status-conscious, impatient, sensitive, overworked, proactive, anxious, and concerned with the proper management of time. Type A personalities are workaholics, they multi-task, particular about finishing work within the deadline, and hate delays as well as ambivalence. These kind of personalities resort to smoking or alcohol abuse as a measure to reduce stress. The three symptoms expressed by Type A behavior include: (1) hostility, which is affected by small issues; (2) impatience and time urgency, which results in exasperation, short-tempered attitude, and irritation; and (3) competitiveness, that drives an individual to stress and an mentality to drive oneself towards continuous achievement.

On the contrary, Type B personalities lead their lives with a lower level of stress as they work at a steady pace and enjoy what they achieve in their lives. People having a type B personality do not suffer from stress when they do not achieve their goals. These are usually creative in nature and enjoy playing with novel concepts and ideas. They often reflect on what is happening around them.

Psychoanalytic theories study human behavior on the basis of the interaction of different components of an individual's personality. Sigmund Freud developed this concept of psychodynamics. The theory of psychodynamics gives importance to dynamic and unconscious conflicts at a psychological level. According to Freud, human personality comprises three elements: the id, ego and superego. The component of id is guided by the principle of pleasure i.e. it demands immediate fulfillment of needs irrespective of the external conditions; the ego appears in order to meet these demands raised by the id, adhering to the principles of the outside world. Lastly, the superego also known as conscience instils moral judgment and the rules of the society on the ego, hence forcing the fulfillment of the demands raised by the id in a realistic as well as a morally correct manner. The superego is developed by the ideals embodied by the parents during the childhood.

The id is an impulsive component that responds immediately to the instinctive demands. It is not affected by logic or reality of the situation. A newborn child possesses the personality of an id that later develops into ego and superego. Whereas the ego engages in a rational, orientated, and realistic approach to problem solving. The superego forms during the age group 3 to 5 years; the function of the superego involves control of the impulsive demands of the id, especially those forbidden by the society. It also persuades the ego to achieve moralistic goals and perfection in each goal. The superego comprises two elements: conscience and ideal self. The conscience can cause a guilty feeling in order to punish the ego if it fulfills immoral demands raised by the id. As a result a person feels bad after committing a wrong action. The element of ideal self is an image of how one sees himself, his career goals, a way of treating others, and appropriate behavior within the society. A person feels guilty if he does not behave according to the ideal self. The superego can also make us feel proud when our demeanor falls in line with the ideal self. The elements of the superego are developed during the childhood based on the values given by the parents and how a child is brought up.

Burrhus Frederic Skinner proposed the **theory of operant conditioning** in order to understand human behavior. This theory stated that you can change behavior by using appropriate reinforcement after the completion of the desired response. Skinner observed three kinds of responses that can affect a person's behavior:

• Neutral operands: Includes responses that do not affect the probability of repeating a particular behavior.

• Reinforcers: Responses increasing the possibility of repeating a particular behavior. Reinforcement is classified as positive or negative. Positive reinforcement involves the association of a reward with a desired behavior that encourages repetition of desirable behavior. Negative reinforcement involves discarding the unpleasant stimulus that helps a person to improve his behavior.

- Punishers: These are responses that reduce the possibility of repeating a behavior. It weakens the personality of an individual.

Now that readers have learned about the various types of personalities and behavioral patterns, it is time to understand the importance of understanding non-verbal communication which will be discussed in the next chapter.

Learning the Art & Secrets of Nonverbal Communication

Peter F Drucker says, "The most important thing in communication is hearing what isn't said." Nonverbal communication forms a substantial part in the process of communication. Nonverbal communication, sometimes mistaken as body language, is defined as a process to send and receive visual signals between people. It creates an impact on the listener along with the outcome. It is truly said, Body language is a very powerful tool. We had body language before we had speech, and apparently, 80% of what you understand in a conversation is read through the body, not the words."

Common examples include a smile, wave, or a wink. All these actions communicate information without using written or oral language. Even silence can effectively communicate the information.

Communication refers to the transfer of information from one person to another. Nonverbal communication is classified into several categories, namely physical, aesthetic, symbols, and signs.

Aesthetic communication occurs when a person expresses the information in a creative way. This type of communication includes music, theatre, dance, crafts, painting, art, and sculpture. For instance, Ballet is a creative representation using music and dance, but no song. An opera uses words, but emphasizes on the facial expressions, posture, costumes, and creative gestures. Physical communication includes personal communication, and focuses on body movements such as a smile or frown, touch, wink, smell, gesture, salute, and many others. Social conversation is a combination of physical signals as well as spoken words.

Signs refer to a mechanical type of nonverbal communication. Examples include 21 gun salute, siren, airplanes display, lights, flags, and many more.

Symbols are a part of the communication process used to imply reasons for personal or religious status, and enhance self esteem. This includes cars, jewelry, clothing, and other items to make others aware about the social status, influence, financial means, or religion of an individual.

Mostly, physical communication is the generally accepted norm by the people. To know a person better, one must understand the nonverbal cues. People can communicate to a large extent by their posture when present among a group of people. The interpretation of the distance maintained between you and the speaker varies across different cultures. It can imply either a sense of attraction, or intensity. Face-to-face interaction implies competition, while side-to side interaction shows cooperation. Posture plays an essential role in nonverbal communication, whether you cross your legs, or fold your arms, or slouch, or stand erect. Touching may convey a feeling of attraction or intimacy. Examples include pat on the back, pushing, hugging, shaking hands, or other ways.

Facial expressions, eye contact, and gestures also play a crucial role in nonverbal communication. For instance, you may roll your eyes to express disinterest. When you are talking to someone, remember that he is noticing the changes in your facial expressions too. Thus, his responses alter accordingly. It is important to maintain eye contact with the speaker to ensure that you are listening to what is being said.

The term 'Paralinguistics' denotes vocal communication apart from the actual language. It comprises voice tone, inflection, loudness, and pitch. When you say something in a strong voice, listeners perceive enthusiasm and approval. If you say something with hesitation, a lack of interest and disapproval is conveyed to the audience.

Kinesics or body language is used to emphasize or reinforce a statement and offers information regarding the attitudes and emotions of an individual. However, it may happen that body movements conflict with the statement. A skilled observer may detect such behavioral discrepancies and use it as a hint to understand other's feelings.

Gestures refer to voluntary or involuntary movements made using different parts of the body, such as hands, legs, arms, fingers, and head. A person with arms crossing over each other demonstrates a sense of insecurity and low confidence. Clenched fist demonstrates anger and stress. Nodding of the head shows your approval to the statement.

The effects of nonverbal communication are:

1. Repetition: Nonverbal cues repeat the message being communicated through actual words.

2. Contradiction:These cues may contradict the message an individual wants to convey.

3. Substitution: The nonverbal cues can effectively substitute a clearly defined verbal message. For example, the eyes of an individual convey a greater vivid message than the actual words spoken.

4. Complementing: Nonverbal cues may complement or add to the meaning of a verbal message. For instance, an employer pats on the back of a deserving employee along with the words, "Well Done. Keep it up!". This combination of verbal as well as nonverbal cues motivates the employee to a greater extent and enhances the impact of the message.

5. Accenting: Nonverbal cues may underline or emphasize a verbal message. An example is the action of pounding your fist on the table to express disagreement or frustration.

Methods & Techniques to Analyze People

1.   Understanding   your   own   value   systems.

A famous psychologist, Eduard Spranger stated that human beings possess six values, the degree varies in each individual. The core values of a human personality include:

- Theoretical value, i.e. passion for knowledge

- Aesthetic value, i.e. a passion for beauty, harmony, and balance

- Social value, i.e. a passion to serve others

- Utilitarian value, i.e. a passion for money and basic utility

- Individualistic value, i.e. a passion for control and power

- Traditional value, i.e. a passion to find highest meaning of life.

The top two values are essential factors to drive an individual and one must fulfill those in order to lead a happy life. If you are aware about your values, you will understand the values of another person accurately and with more clarity.

2.   Understand the values of the other person

Suppose your topmost value is another person's lowest value, you will definitely face misunderstandings as well as end up in conflicts with the other person. Once you understand the value system of the other person, you will be able to improve your communication with the other individual.

3.   Awareness about your Differences.

Conflicts arise when the values of an individual are different from the other person's set of values. For instance, if you have a Theoretical approach, i.e. you give importance to the value of knowledge. Thus, you solve problems using an analytical approach and arrive at rationally justified decisions. If another person has an Aesthetic approach means he believes in the artistic situations of life and arrives at emotional decisions. Therefore, both of you will have a conflict . This difference of opinion is also termed as the conflict between the right brain and the left brain or between the head and the heart. So, you should understand the differences between the value systems and resolve your differences.

4. Let people be themselves.

Each person has a different passion and motive of leading life. We must appreciate the point of view or opinions of other people being less judgmental about it. It is truly said, "We don't see things as they are, we see them as we are."

5. Clear boundaries should be set.

It is obvious that in order to improve or sustain a relationship, you should not allow people to criticize any aspect of your personality. A relationship is like two sides of a coin. Usually, when people start to feel that you understand them completely, they will appreciate your association and will understand you better. You should make things clear to others as to how they should treat you.

6. Platinum Rule.

The Platinum Rule says, "Do unto others as they would have you do unto them." If you behave with people in the manner which you want them to behave in, it may not conform to their values. It does not matter if people have varied priorities or beliefs. If you wish that people should give respect to your attitudes and values, you must also respect theirs.

7.   Respect   yourself   as   well   as   others

When you are aware about the differences of the other person and the reason behind it, you will enjoy an improved communication and develop a compatible relationship with the other person.

Fritz Heider, the founder of the Attribution theory, based his theory on the causes of different behavioral patterns in a human being. People want to know the reasons for their actions as well as the actions of others; they attribute causes to certain patterns of behavior instead of assuming that these are random behaviors. As a result, people assume authoritative control over own behaviors and situations.

Attribution refers to a process comprising three stages. In the first stage, an individual's behavior is observed. In the second stage, the perceiver has to determine that the observed pattern of behavior is deliberate in nature. It means that the person who is being observed must be assumed to behave intentionally. In the third and the final stage, the observer relates the observed pattern of behavior to causes that may either be internal or external. Internal causes are attributes associated with the person who is being observed, whereas external causes are the attributes associated with external factors or outside environment. Internal attributions refer to a person's capability or the outcome determined by the efforts of a person. Luck and task difficulty can serve as the external causes of certain behavior. When you are perceiving the behavior in such cases, a judgment should be made taking into consideration the respective factor that has led to the particular behavior. The elements of consistency, distinctiveness as well as consensus play an equally important role in determining the causes of behavior pattern.

Consistency refers to a situation to determine whether the individual under observation behaves in a similar way when he faces the similar set of situations or circumstances. If there is no change in the individual's behavior under similar conditions, the level of consistency is termed as high; if he behaves in a different manner each time, then the level of consistency will be regarded as low. Distinctiveness is a state to determine whether the individual being observed behaves in the similar fashion at different kinds of situations. If no change occurs in the behavioral pattern under a variety of situations, then the person is less distinctive; if different behavior is exhibited at different situations, then the person is highly distinctive. The last element of the attribute theory, consensus refers to the degree of how similar people, if under similar situations, would behave in relation to the person who is being observed. If other people act in the similar pattern, it is a situation involving a high consensus. However, if other people behave in a different manner depending on the situation, the situation will have a low consensus.

People associate attributions to the daily activities. A major problem is associating attributes to the cause is the fundamental attribution error, i.e. a tendency to overestimate the effect personal factors have on one's behavior and underestimate the way situational factors can influence an individual's behavior.

Frequently asked questions

Psychologists study individual behavior using the medium of personality tests, i.e. a questionnaire or other standardized instrument designed to reveal specific aspects of an individual's character.

The period of 1920s saw the inception of personality tests being used for selecting personnel for the armed forces. Examples of such personality tests include the Myers Briggs Type Indicator (MBTI), the Minnesota Multiphasic Personality Inventory (MMPI), and various other personality tests based on the Five Factor Model. Personality tests are applied in varied contexts, although not limited to, such as individual counseling, career counseling, occupational health and safety, relationship counseling, and customer interaction management.

Various kinds of rating scales have been developed to measure the attitude of an individual accurately. The most popular rating scale to be used is the Likert scale. The

Likert scale, developed in 1932, is a linear continuum ranging from strongly agree to strongly disagree; it measures the individual's attitude by the responses given by people to a specific set of questions related to a topic, as to what extent they agree with the subject, and studying the affective as well as cognitive components of an individual's attitude. The Likert Scale has 5 or even 7 rating points, allows the individual to express as to what extent they disagree or agree with a specified statement or topic.

The Thematic Apperception Test, commonly known as TAT is effective in extracting information about an individual's view about the world and personal attitudes towards self and the others. Participants of TAT are shown many story picture cards and they need to tell stories related to the images. They express their expectations and feelings about relationships with parents, peers, or other individuals, and probable romantic partners. The examiner assesses the content of the story along with the mannerisms, posture, vocal tone, hesitations, and other emotional signs exhibited by the participant while telling about a particular picture. For instance, a person feeling anxious after seeing a certain image may comment on its artistic style, or make a remark that she or he doesn't like it; thereby avoiding telling a story related to that picture.

Along with individual assessment, the TAT is applied for studying about the specific aspects of individual personality basically, the need for achievement, fear about failure, aggression and hostility, and interpersonal relationships with objects. Studies about interpersonal object relations using the TAT involve examination of diverse topics such as the extent of emotional involvement in relationships; the capability of individuals to understand the complex situations of human relationships; the ability to differentiate between the individual viewpoint and others' perspectives about a particular situation; the ability of individuals to control aggression and negative impulses; issues related to self esteem as well as personal identity.

The personality test of Myers–Briggs Type Indicator (MBTI) is a psychometric questionnaire specially designed to study psychological preferences as to how people think about the world and arrive at a decision. Carl Jung developed a psychological theory which acted as the foundation of the personality test of the Myers–Briggs Type Indicator. He proposed that two pairs of dichotomous cognitive functions existing in human beings include:

- The judging/rational functions that involve feeling and thinking
- The perceiving/irrational functions that involve intuition and sensation.

Jung believed each function is expressed by an individual in either its extroverted form or an introverted form. The typological model suggested by Carl Jung considers psychological type of an individual as similar to right or left handedness, i.e. people possesses certain preferred ways of thinking and decision-making. These ways are either determined by birth, or an individual develops these ways by his experiences. The MBTI classifies these differences into dichotomies, or four opposite pairs that give a researcher an option of studying 16 different types of human psychology. These types cannot be rated as better or worse; the MBTI theory considers that individuals usually prefer an overall combination including all the type differences. Similarly, a right-handed individual finds it hard to write with the left hand; so people find it difficult to use their dichotomous psychological preferences, even though they can develop a flexible behavior with a little practice.

The 16 psychological types are generally termed as an abbreviation including four letters i.e. the first letters of each type preference; the only exception being the use of letter N for intuition, as I am generally used for introversion. For instance:

The type ESTJ means an individual possessing the characteristics of extraversion (E), sensing (S), thinking (T), and judgment (J). The abbreviation INFP denotes an individual possessing the characteristics of introversion (I), intuition (N), feeling (F0, and perception (P).

The Minnesota Multiphasic Personality Inventory (MMPI) is a psychometric personality test that has gained worldwide recognition. This standardized test is used to study psychopathology and adult personality. Psychologists use various forms of the test to devise treatment plans; help differential diagnosis; answer legal questions related to forensic psychology; screen candidates during the recruitment process; or while conducting therapeutic assessments.

This kind of personality assessment test is currently administered in either of the two forms — the MMPI-2, including a set of 567 true or false questions, and the newer version of MMPI-2-RF, including 338 questions that need be to stated as true or false. While the latter is an advanced measure, it is completed in half the time and has become popular due to its research base as well as familiarity with mental health professionals. The MMPI-A is another version of the personality test, and is specially designed for the teenagers.

Conclusion

Judging an individual's personality is not a complex process. We simply need to remember the small things in order to understand an individual.

Through this EBook, readers have got an insight on how to understand the behavior and the personality of an individual in an effective manner. Readers have become aware about the various types of personalities existing in this world. They also get an idea of observing the unspoken attributes of communication and how it affects the process of understanding a person. Reading this EBook, people have learnt about the various effects of creating a good first impression by adopting the proper demeanor. It is rightly said, "Beauty only gets attention. Personality is what captures the heart."

Before you analyze people, it is important that you learn the art of effective listening. Simply follow the steps mentioned in this EBook to hone the skills of a good listener. The readers get an idea about the various types of personalities as well as how important it is to understand the correct type of personality of an individual in order to analyze people. The different patterns of behavior, its causes, and effects of behavior have been highlighted in this EBook. The readers get an insight on how to study the various patterns of behavior that are being exhibited by an individual, while judging his personality. People should not jump into conclusions about a person's behavior; rather, they should try to understand the circumstances that led to a person develop the particular kind of behavior pattern.

This EBook also gives certain tips and methods which a person can adopt in order to understand people. Different theories related to learning and personality have been highlighted in this book to help people understand others' behavior and adjust with them accordingly to lead a happy life. Happiness and personal satisfaction are the ultimate goals of an individual's life. These goals can be easily achieved if a person follows the philosophy of "Live, and let others live". Ultimately, this requires an accurate understanding of the personality of other individuals in the community so that all people can coexist and live their lives amicably. A person who develops a good understanding of analyzing people will be favored in the business circle as well as the social circle.

I wish that all the readers will take a leaf out of this EBook and attempt to understand people around them effectively. Thank You!

Made in the USA
San Bernardino, CA
14 September 2015